LAST HEAT

by Peter Blair

Winner of the 1999 Washington Prize

THE WORD WORKS
WASHINGTON, D.C.

Book design, typography by Janice Olson
Cover design by Janice Olson

Cover photograph: Charging hot metal into an open-hearth fur-
        nace, Open-Hearth 5, Homestead Steel Works.
        Frontispiece: Ore yard of #6 and #7 furnaces, Carrie
        Furnace, Homestead Steel Works. All photos courtesy of the
        William J. Gaughan Collection, Archives Service Center,
        University of Pittsburgh.

Production management: Marta Levcheva
Printed in Bulgaria

Library of Congress Number: 99-72869
International Standard Book Number: 0-915380-44-7

Acknowledgments

Apalachee Quarterly: "Ripsy"; *The And Review*: "My Father and I Wait For Deer"; *The Bassettown Review*: "The Night We Pitch It"; *Crazyhorse*: "Coke Man" and "Track Boss"; *In Pittsburgh*: "Vacation At Sassafras Cabin, 1965"; *The Listening Eye*: "Fatality, Open-Hearth 5" and "Track Gang"; *Mobius*: "Smoke," "Ohio Underworld," and "Sharpsville Quality Product Mill"; *Pittsburgh Post-Gazette*: "What Love Is"; *The Pittsburgh Quarterly*: "Carrie Furnace," "'Company' John," "It's My Job," and "Beneficiation"; *Poem*: "Kitchen Surgery"; *Poems & Plays*: "What it Takes," "Slag Pit," "Quitting Time At Homestead Steel," and "Trudging Through the Ore Yard Looking For the Supervisor's Balls"; *Poetic Page/Opus*: "Luna" and "The Shipping Floor"; *River City*: "Wing Damage"; *West Branch*: "Uniform."

"Number 6 and 7 Furnaces," "Phoenix," "Hazelwood Angel," "August Twilight Near the Hot-Metal Bridge" and "Dust" appeared in *Furnace Greens*, a chapbook (Defined Providence Press, 1998 contest winner).

"Furnace Labor," "Changing Rolls On the Universal Mill," "Bronco," "Visiting Slovan, Pa." and "Heckman and Cooley" appeared in *A Round, Fair Distance From the Furnace*, a chapbook (White Eagle Coffee Store Press, 1993 contest winner).

"Furnace Greens" and "Trudging Through the Ore Yard Looking For the Supervisor's Balls" won Honorable Mention and Finalist, respectively, in the 1995 National Writers Union Contest, Philip Levine, judge.

•

In "Wing Damage," lines 47-48 are from the Navy accident report, and lines 51-54 are an eye-witness account of the crash.

•

I am grateful to the Pennsylvania Council On the Arts for poetry fellowships which aided in the completion of many of these poems.

I'd like to thank Rina Ferrarelli, Alice Fuchs, Foster Provost, and especially, Elizabeth Gargano, for their assistance and careful reading of many of these poems.

Thanks to David Rosenberg, the Labor Archivist at Hillman Library, and to Miriam Meislik, Photo Curator at the Archives Service Center, University of Pittsburgh.

Heartfelt thanks to William J. Gaughan for sharing his memories and insights about Homestead Steel, without which some of these poems could not have been written.

CONTENTS

I. FATHERS

II. BROTHERS

For my parents Joseph R. Blair and Margaret M. Blair

For my brother Steven Blair

For the thousands of men and women who worked at Homestead Steel

Power house and trestle, Carrie Furnace

1

FATHERS

The Past isn't dead. It isn't even past.

—WILLIAM FAULKNER

Number 6 and 7 Furnaces

They tower by the river,
iron and brick beakers,
rust-brown as lava rocks,
silent, hollow, saved for a time
from the scrap heap. Trees
grow from their blow stacks.

One night when these furnaces still burned
two men lay on the tracks,
heads against the rail under a coal car.
They were fixing the brakes,
and forgot to clamp the red metal warning flags
to the rails. A diesel engine heading
through darkness didn't stop.
When it hit the coal car,
the wheels rolled over their necks,
clean and vicious as a guillotine's blade.
Their wives got the call
from the union rep and the night shift
shattered forever.

Today in Pittsburgh, the horizon's free
of stacks and cast houses
except for these broken stumps
sticking impudently above the hills.
Now the city calls them: *Minimal
Secured Ruins*. The other furnaces
have been bulldozed and flattened.

Most people have forgotten
how they stained the river mud with acid
and poured their two cents of steel
into the Manhattan skyline.

On Pittsburgh's South Side
an abandoned steel mill collapses
across Carson Street, crushes cars,
blocks traffic for days.
In Monesson, when they dynamite the mill,
it covers its town in soot one last time.
An angry woman kicks at the grit
scarring her cement walkway,
That'll never come out.
Maybe she's remembering
the sooty sidewalks of her childhood,
mill-dust on her father's tomatoes,
his shirt collars, his window sills.

Now a loose tin panel creaks
and bangs against the cast house wall.
The ore yard sprouts jagged weeds,
alive with grasshoppers. The wind
hoots across the furnace tops
like a child blowing on an empty bottle.
Maybe they'll make a museum here.
We can approach the furnaces
from the river. We can touch
their cold iron skin.
We can leave flowers.

Furnace Greens

I bumped along Braddock Avenue
under dripping bridges, past glowering casements
of Union Switch and Signal. I turned
before the Rankin Bridge, circled down
the spiral ramp to the river
and the twisted pipes of six blast furnaces.

I was a man in furnace greens
and an orange hard hat, my shadow cast
in fluorescent light, moonlight and flowing light
of hot iron. My shadow fell
into pits, across metal grids, stretched
hundreds of feet down to the ore yard
from the high catwalks of ovens.

I breathed in diesel fumes, sinter dust,
and the metallic steam wisping off slag.
The earth smoked under my feet. The sky burned
with orange clouds. The night river gleamed
like a coal seam. I ate on ledges, piers,
and in steel sheds. I spoke the rough staccato:
*working hard, sweeping up, screw this job,
you're all right* — the cynicism of machines,
the black humor of grease and bruises.

I learned the pick and shovel, the sledge,
the post-hole digger, and the jack hammer.
I kept company with cranes,

backhoes, sheers, presses, and vats of acid.
My hands became steel hooks; my arms,
10 cables; my joints, chain links.
My eyes turned into glass, plastic,
and wire mesh. I saw a man lose fingers
when a lift-chain crushed them against steel plates.
I saw a hot strip of sheet metal jump the rolls
and sidewind across the floor
like a red snake. I saw the full moon rippled
into rags of light above a furnace stack.

I did the mill slouch, my boot up
on a stack of slabs, my forearms on my knee,
sitting without a chair, leaning
without a wall, looking like I didn't care.
I drove home with explosions
ringing in my ears, my lips blackened by soot,
eyebrows and nose hairs singed.
Army vets would fit right in. They knew the slang,
the smoldered deference to authority,
the snicker and snort as the foreman left
the room. They knew it was war.

I was a mystery to the men, reading Wordsworth
on the third floor of the Sinter Plant.
I looked out at the poisoned river,
oily and green as anti-freeze, closed in
by mills around both bends, closed in
by the whistle, swing shifts, and fumes.
I thought that nature had died.

The men mistook my anger for fuddlement,
my dreaminess, for weak knees.
We watched each other, pretending
we weren't taking it all into our hearts:
the river locks, stock-piled ore,
and barrel-chested furnaces pumping their smoke
into Pittsburgh's gray clouds.

Smoke

All I remember is fighting, Smoke says,
one day sitting on a bench between casts.
So far he never talks much to me
when I clean out the runners, or help him
changing stoves. I'm surprised. To him
I'm just a white, middle-class kid,
over-eager, awed by the mill. He tells me
he was the only black deck hand on the river,
when bare white knuckles came at his face
in the iron holds of ore barges.

He'd block roundhouses, uppercuts,
peering out through his fists and forearms,
bobbing his head, jabbing to keep distance,
until the man tired. Then he'd explode,
pounding the man's chest, stomach, kidneys,
not to mark him up, but so he'd feel it
in his guts: *Takes away the legs
and the wind.* The other men, and those
he'd beaten, jeered from the gunwales
until the challenger dropped his hands.
Smoke says he promised to quit the river
the day one of those *white-meats* beat him.

After five years and twenty-some fights
he signed on at Carrie Furnace for better pay.
He stares straight ahead, the daylight glowing
like a blow torch outside the cast house vents

reflected in his eyes. His words drift down
from somewhere a tap explosion has scattered them
years ago. His chest heaves slowly,
an old furnace, a molten story. *How many blacks*
do you see on the river, even today?
I was their sport, see? That was the Forties.
All I remember is fighting. When the foreman calls us
for the next cast, the light in his eyes
vanishes, nothing there now but gray smoke.

Phoenix

Some mornings I imagine
the corrugated roofs of the cast house
unfolding in the gray air,
dark, sheet metal wings
lifting off from
the furnace's bottom-heavy belly.

Every shift, the cast house
fires up orange, flickering
out of its own ashes. Half the workers
have motorcycles; half, mortgages.

I imagine the fluted, stacked roofs
caught in time-lapse, flapping
higher, like me to another job,
another town, another river.

'Ski says, *The money's good.*
He's young. But Smoke warns,
Stay out of this shit.
Only thing you get here is crazy.

Some mornings I imagine
the gabled roofs of the cast house
shrinking in the gray air,
the fluted, winged roofs
folding up, snuffing
the orange casting-light
to iron, to cold heavy iron.

Hazelwood Angel

As a kid I knew they were pouring heats
by the orange flicker on low-lying clouds.
I learned to listen for the mill whistle

at noon and four droning through the crack of bats
on wiffle balls all summer. At midnight,
its long, hoarse groan whispered at my window.

Half asleep after prayers, I imagined
an angel had lost her way among stacks,
calling, *Home*. White, ethereal, she rose

like a cloud of steam from the Hazelwood
coke ovens. Her dress billowed above hills
as the doused, hot coke cooled. Soon

her body thinned, and the river wind
ripped her apart. The night Uncle Frank died,
I dreamed his spirit rose from his doused flesh

to float high over the Glenwood Bridge.
His burn-scarred arms reached for me. His Greek voice
rasped through a haze of smoke and mist.

It was the whistle, of course, that could not
find its way past the dark, fine hairs rimming
his cold ears, and reluctantly found mine.

Black Snow

Aunt Mary smoothes her flowered apron
in the door of her downstairs apartment.
My father won't speak to her, ushers us
through the dark lobby and up the steps
to his other sister, Aunt Sophie, and Grandma Blair.

We sip hot cocoa by steamed windows. Outside,
the stacks of Hazelwood coke ovens loom through snow
above Bates Street. Mary must hear us pounding
the floorboards above her, running from Uncle Gus' tickles.
Grandma Blair pats our darting heads,

her jaw clamped tight, her smile thin as wire.
Sophie wraps the strudel Grandma made
for my father, her *Slivovitza*, her doctor son.
They disappear for an hour. My father's in the bedroom,
pushing in my grandmother's hemorrhoids.

I've heard the story. Mary threw Grandma out
of her spare room, got tired of her nagging,
whispering, *Why can't your Frank keep a job?*
We sit by the back door, draw pictures in window fog,
watch dark, sooty snow build up on the sills.

Who's to blame for the black snow?
Ash blows over the frozen ground. We're leaving.
Running to the car, Mickey and I shove to get in first.
Mary watches from her window, holding up
the lace curtain. Steve says, *Dad, she's waving.*

You don't see her, he answers, chipping ice
off the windshield. Her hand drops to her side.
The white lace falls together, hiding Mary
on that day in the Fifties, when we kids drifted
through those hallways, indifferent as snow.

Kitchen Surgery

When a hammer blow bloodies my fingernail,
I keep throwing wet snowballs all next day,
giving the infection a chance, the purple
fingertip swelling. So my father tapes my hand
to the kitchen table, injects Novocain
into the base of the finger, touches it:
Can you feel that? I grab the table edge
and look away at the row of black pan handles
hanging on the opposite wall. With the first cut
only blood flows out over the nail,
so he makes a second. When he asks if it hurts,
I call loudly and slowly to the walls,
It's not too bad. My mother puts her arms
around my shoulders, siphoning off some
of the wild static. After the third cut he says,
There it is! I steal a glance and see yellow
oozing among red. *But I thought there'd be more,*
he says, bandages it, and gives me aspirin.
Maybe I didn't use enough Novocain. His eyes ask
for reassurance. Not knowing how much Novocain
a man would need, I say, *It'll be fine,*
and go upstairs where the real pain rushes in,
like waves, with no father watching.

Bronco

After steaks at the Farm Family Diner,
my father drives his Chevy wagon,
swaying like a horse's backside
onto Braddock Avenue's chipped asphalt.
A Bronco speeds right, passes us
in the gap between parked cars, cuts
my father off. *Son of a bitch,* he growls,
my mother beside him, five kids in back.

He floors the gas, catches the guy, beeps,
blinks his brights. A stallion leaps
on black vinyl covering the spare, a lone
capped silhouette at the wheel. The Bronco slows.
We barely miss his tail light as my father swerves
across the yellow dividing line. He passes him,
thumbing his nose. Near Dallas Avenue,
a horn blares behind us: the Bronco.

I'm scared now, but Steve says, *We can take him,
Dad.* In the rear-view my father's eyes shift
from the road to the mirror. Beeps staccato
behind us. *He'll follow us home,* my mother says.
Above us, a black net of electric wires
stretches across the dark sky.

We pull to the curb. The Bronco stops
behind us. Green traffic light smears
on our hood. *You're not getting out of this*

car, Joe! my mother says. *All you have to do
is stay calm,* he snarls into the mirror
and opens his door half-way. The interior light
switches on, and a ski jacket stalks
through our pale children's faces
reflected in the windows. My father slams his door,
roars through a red light, the man shrinking
in our back window. We turn, zigzag side streets,
park in front of someone else's house.

One hand on the wheel, my father sighs.
Ditched him. He drives past yellow porch lights
that turn front steps into shining ladders.
But the Bronco prowls two blocks ahead,
stops, backs up. I'm thrown against the left door.
Parked cars whiz by on Barnsdale, Woodwell, Kinsman.
My father circles crazily: *We're going straight
home.* He cuts his lights on Linden,
squeals onto Edgerton, and slips into the garage.

My mother walks fast to the back door, muttering:
Stupid, stupid, stupid! My father's sheepish.
His hands shake putting the key into the car lock,
but he manages a smile for Steve,
who says, *You made a clean getaway, Dad.*
We've seen all the Westerns, the Duke movies,
so we don't think about the random bad guy
looming out of nowhere. We haven't learned
a getaway is never clean. My father
has a patient in labor that night, a mastectomy
scheduled in the morning. He keeps an M-1
cleaned and loaded under his bed.

Fifteen minutes later, I walk the dog,
turn a corner. The Bronco
moves up Linden, checking cars, driveways.
All I have to do is stay calm.

Vacation at Sassafras Cabin, 1965

The dirt biker hunting rattlesnakes
spatters down our road. On the radio,
electric guitars complain to the rustling
trees outside: *I Can't Get No*
Satisfaction. But I get it, hammering
tongue-and-groove floorboards
into place, skilsawing roof beams,
hearing the high-pitched yelps of nails
going in. Laying electric wires
even to the outhouse, my father transforms
the cabin from the 18th to the 20th
century, that summer before high school.
Before the cook at the Wagon Wheel
pushes through the swinging door
waving a kitchen knife: *I don't serve*
long-haired males like your son. Before
I yell in my father's face that napalm
on a child's body never stops
burning. That summer I still adore
his language: *Get a good purchase*
on that joist. And when I crowbar
the fat two-by-six into its solid housing,
he can still whisper, *Good soldier*.

Beneficiation

Beneficiation: controlled burning of iron ore
to make it a desirable feed for a blast furnace

3 days at the Sinter Plant, I'm sweeping
and Dangerous Dan roars: *Did you*
turn down the nozzles on #5? I nod, mumble
something about too much flow.
I've watched # 5 conveyor, an elongated snake,
exposed insides glowing orange.
Water streams against upward-moving iron coals
that hiss and steam on its rippling rubber.
At belt's end the coals leap out like a red tongue.
Who told you to monkey with those nozzles?
He curses me, blowing out exasperation
like a blast furnace's flue pipes.
We cross a catwalk, two stairs, and I see # 5,
the longest belt, descending, its rubber skin bubbled,
pocked. *That's $2000 gone!* Dan yells.
Elbows on the railing, I lean toward the charred belt.
What made me turn down the sprays that quenched
those glowing coals? That spring,
I'd graduated high school. My father insisted
the mill would make me a man.
But Uncle Frank had warned, *Steel mill's no good*
for you. He'd tended furnace at J & L.
Dan slaps the railing with his gloves.
Next time, before you do anything, ask!
It's the last I hear of it,
except the men call me *nozzle* all summer.

It's My Job

When Charlie tells us to clean the soaking pits,
Quarles whispers: *Too many old heads messin'*
with our minds. His hands twitch, as if shaking off
water drops. Most days Charlie keeps us busy
sweeping up. Nights we sleep a few hours
on benches by the lockers. Now we strap asbestos spats
over our boots and furnace greens, shove our hands
into the hard felt of fire-resistant gloves,
gauntleted to the elbows. *Let's go, you first.*
We enter a dark corridor of glowing slits.
Behind iron doors, steel ingots soak in gas jets
until they're soft enough for the rollers
to squeeze into slabs. A cherry-picker lifts a door.
The glow grows from the floor up, a wall
of heat. I hold a glove to my cheeks, curl up
behind the crane-wheel like paper on a hearth.
Get over there! Charlie yells. *It's your job.*
I stare blankly, all coward. He has to show me.
A disgusted father, his face vanishes
behind the back of his hand, grabbing
a long rake-bar. *With all that asbestos*
you could walk through hell. He strides to the glare,
turns a shoulder to three haloed ingots
rippling in the oven, hard hat cocked to shield
his ungoggled eyes. His leather cheeks glow.
Always take your time, he says through dust
and sulfuric fumes. With smooth strokes
he heaves the long rake in, pulls hot slag out,

lets the bar's end fall to the dirt each time.
Now you. I take the bar, step to the heat.
I stagger, heave it, rest it. The air sears my lungs.
I can't stand it much longer, trying to separate the heat
from my fear of the heat. I whisper, *five rakes,*
see what it takes, now six, now seven, eight's late,
nine's fine, ten screws, no way out but to dance
with the deadly heat along the oven front,
a rhythm to time my breaths. *That's it.*
Send in Quarles. The cable lowers the dark door,
cutting off the glare like a merciful guillotine.
I drag my feet to the exit. Quarles says, *You okay,*
red face? No sweat, I say, and it's true.
I'm baked dry. My turn will come again
in twenty minutes or less. *You'll get used*
to it, bro', Quarles says. His favorite phrase.

What Love Is

Across the kitchen table, we fight again.
I shout, *It's MY future,* leave the steak
my father grilled for me. Stomping up the steps,
I think of the veins bulging on his forehead,
the white collar he so desired tight around his neck.
Hungry, I sit on the landing, listen to him
gripe to my mother: *The world won't
treat him half as well.* From my height,
I watch him enter sunlight in the front hall,
peeling the foil off a small chocolate egg,
silent, meticulous. Glimmers of pity
fleck the white plaster, and wooden
floorboards, rising up through my disdain
solid as the house. Later, I go back down
to the kitchen, past the banister-posts
marking this stairway of lost chances.
He's slicing pears by the stove.
Our mean words linger like cooking smells
in the air between us. I mumble, *I'm not going
upstairs anymore.* His back muscles shake
under the knit shirt. Cut, cut, he works the blade,
jiggling his belted belly, pressed
against the counter. He turns, comes at me,
the knife still tight in his fist. Its flash
circles my head as we embrace.

Coke Man

For two weeks I draw lucky, coke man
on #4. Alone, I work outside atop the trestle,
halfway up the furnace's round rusted body.
I can see the river, the sky. The other side
of the furnace glows and rumbles,
the cast house, none of my business
as long as I keep feeding coke
to the wide-mouthed hopper under the tracks,
and venture into the deep high coal cars
to shovel out the last coke piled in dents.
I never see the castmaster or any white hats,
just the brakeman from Union Railroad
when I call for a new four-car fix
of black rocks, hard as pumice, light
as wiffle balls. After I sledge hammer
the bottom doors open, the coke tumbles,
fills the hopper. The car drains
slowly. I get a half-hour break. Time
to watch the skip cars climb the furnace
and dump their loads. Nights are best,
as low summer moons cut through clouds
over the Monongahela. I imagine Indians
and French soldiers paddling upriver
to give the British their worst defeat
in the New World. One morning, Orion
melts into the dawn, and a white bird
flies from thick river mist, circles
high over Homestead. *Your cars set
for awhile?* Mr. Appleby, a supervisor, asks.

Surprised, I nod. He motions for me
to sit with him on a rail, our steel-toed boots
between the ties. He takes off his white hat,
drops his safety glasses into it: *Where're you from?*
Red rings circle his eyes. He talks 10 minutes
about how most men don't appreciate the equipment:
the incredible enterprise the mill really is.
He places his hand on my shoulder, grips
and shakes me. *But you do. You're not like
most of these guys.* His round fleshy face
smiles with fatherly eyes. *You like
working coke man?* Maybe he just wants talk,
someone who won't call him *asshole*
behind his back, someone who's new,
not beaten down by this incredible enterprise
at war with the men who keep it going.
Maybe he wants a warm body
to listen among caverns of empty coke cars
and hoppers ceaselessly rumbling beneath
the trestle like hungry prisoners, so near
and so far from the river. But fear, orange
as my hard hat, that I'll spend each morning
alone with him: informant, suck-up, boyfriend,
fear overcomes me. *It's boring. You see more
on the furnace.* He takes his hand away
doesn't believe me. The coke's gone
from the car behind us. *What were you looking at
when I came?* I say, *God-damn quitting time.*
Nothing to do but grab the hook
and safety belt, climb the high wall
of the coke car. Next week I'm in the cast
house, shoveling hot iron from the runners.

Furnace Labor

Liquid red iron races hot
down the runners, cools
to sluggish silver, crusts
into immobility.
Sweating, we sledge it,
and shovel the hot chunks
into wheel barrows.
The boards we stand on
to protect our shoes flame up
under our soles.
Once I crouch too low
to the iron, lift,
and dump. A white light
hugs the furnace greens
around my knee and thigh
like sunlight shafting
into the cast house. Misty
and liquid, the gleams
thicken, unearthly blue
water rising. It takes me
a few seconds
to realize I'm burning.

Ripsy

He grabs my elbow at the sandwich machines.
The chipped ham on rye gleams
behind its glass door, wrapped tight
in cellophane, the only thing in the mill
free of soot and grease. *Show you something?*
I follow him between the furnaces.
With each step, he totters, hitches
his shoulders, like a wobbly tire.
Among valves, stanchions, and the cramped
metal girths of the ovens, he picks up
a two-by-four behind a huge pipe
that hisses like lost breath searching
for a pair of lungs. *Hit me with this,*
he says. He takes off his hard hat.
On the side of my head, here. It began
with the shakes, he says. Then one day
the furnace moved, reaching for him
with its black pipes, and he emptied his flask
into the hopper, but it always got filled
again. *I'm drinking myself to death
on this job.* I should have dropped the board,
walked away. But his face: shrunken,
three rivulets creased around his mouth.
He'd stood by the open hopper for years
clearing the grid of caked ore,
drizzle blowing in off the river. *Do it.*
I take the board in both hands, *Why me?*
You're young. They'll believe you.

He stares up at the sky cut off
by the curved oven domes
that haven't shut down for 20 years.
I bring it down on his temple.

For days I tell the men, the supervisors,
the board fell off a catwalk.
I hit my own head in private, raise a lump.
I almost lose two fingers
hooking up a hoist. They transfer me
to a labor gang across the river.
I never see him again except in dreams.
The thick board glances off his skull
with a sick *thunk*, my wrists stinging
and numb. Still smiling, wide-eyed,
he crumples. I lay his head on the cement.
Blood seeps through his hair,
unconscious as a river. It's raining.
In the dream no one comes to save him.
No one gives him disability.
In the dream he's my grandfather.

Track Boss

In blue work clothes, a Royal Crown decal
stuck to his hard hat, he looks like a king,
riding the tracks on his pump cart
among picks, shovels and spikes. His chosen
one or two ride with him while we laborers
train after, chasing down the bent, weak rails,
changing rotted ties, watching ladle cars
full of molten iron sag the gravel-bed
and lift rusted spikes out of the wood.
He's taught us to hammer in tandem:
one strikes the spike-head as another wrist-
pivots the peened sledge over his shoulders
and clinks it down, alternating hits,
until the spike-lip kisses the chink
of rail flange. Once, he grabs a hammer
in each hand, drives a spike home
amid swirling steel heads. *That's*
when you get good, Angel says. He lost
two toes before steel-topped boots were law
in the mill, but we didn't find that out
from him. As we pass, men wave wistfully
atop the cast house floor or lean
from dark doors in corrugated tin walls.
They call: *Hey, Happy Jack, lord*
of the tracks, or *He's big, he's mean*
he's clean. It always seems that dust
clings to our faces and clothes, not his.

He nods, tips the point of his track gauge
toward them, a speared scepter, yells, *Damn
George, you're looking old.* Changing ties
he works his share, picking to my shovel,
shoveling to Bob's pick: *You don't work
your share, you don't work with me.*
We all want the steady days.
Just once he let Angel sleep one off an hour.
We heard him stand off an angry foreman
who wanted to pull Angel to first helper
on the furnace. *I need every man I have,*
he yelled flourishing the pointed gauge,
and they sparred over who out-ranked
the other. *This gang's a team. You run
the cast house like a prison.* The foreman turned.
Yeah, he said to the sky, walking away,
and I'm the fucking warden. That
was something. Most days Jack waltzes
out the gate at half-past the whistle
after a long shower and friendly bull
with other 20-year men. At 5 to, I enter the crowd
each day in the tunnel and shove past the guard,
who can hardly take our time cards from us,
we give them up so fast. Maybe the girth
of his rounded biceps and belly
coaxes time to orbit him as the moon
circles the earth, even as the earth keeps
its round, fair distance from the furnace
of the sun. One morning, fixing a switch
behind the Sinter Plant, he disappears

on break, down into the riverbank's lush
growth. Five, ten minutes, we wait.
Shaking a dump, Angel says. Climbing
from the brush, sweat-darkened underarms
and chest, he rises, each hand clutching a bunch
of thick greens: *I'm frying these up
tonight and none of you is invited.*
He binds them, lays them in the spike box,
clumps of black dirt clinging to the roots.

My Father And I Wait For Deer

Twilight, our rear ends cold
against opposite fenders
of his Chevy Wagon, we stare
into the dense, darkening
green. I turn

to the shape I was molded from.
His canvas cap and square frame
thicken against limbs
tangling flecks of last light.
He offers

low comments, designed
for the present task: *Evening
is the time they walk, I know,*
as the deep lake's surface reveals
only what it's always been
all these years.

Now the lake sinks the darkening sky
into its own deep light.
In gray air, we crane
toward each

rustle in the leaves. It's okay
that no deer come.

Changing Rolls On the Universal Mill

When the top roll breaks,
Charlie knows by the rumble thudding
the hot mill air, reaching
our cement ledge near the rail tracks
and river trees: *Gonna
be a fun afternoon.*

Inside, the white hats
come down from the pulpit,
point at the steaming stand.
The roll's cracked cylinder hangs askew
like two terrible teeth
the ingot has punched loose.

Back from a huddle of inspection teams,
with trouble lights and tool belts,
Charlie says, *Got to go in.*
The overhead crane creaks forward
through upper darkness, dangling
its steel talons.

First we undress her.
We unscrew each spindle,
release the coupling boxes, hook
and unhook until *all clear*
above the broken roll. *Whose turn?*
Quarles says, *I went last time.*
Jeff's too fat. John's off sick.
Okay Blair, you're it.

I crawl on boards laid over the rolls,
ease my ankles into dark spaces.
Above me, the cable hook swings
lower, closer. Inside
the stand's sweltering chamber,
I worm to the sawed-off, barrel-round chunk,
touch its fire-cracks with a glove,
feel its warm breath.

Between vertical rolls
that could labor me like a hot ingot
into one dimension,
I inch my shoulders up. Bearings
ooze grease. Water drips.
Chains cling tense to gears.
On my belly, I grab the hook,
yell to the crane. No one hears.
Nowhere to look but up
into the steep well of the machine shafts,
past girders and darkness
to the halogen stars.

Inside the universal mill
I fit my body to the curves and teeth
its operators never see.

That machine turns us all
in its cogs & gears. I feel its loneliness,
wonder how I'll go back on break
to my chipped ham sandwich
and warm Coke black as grease,
the men joking & complaining.

Lower it! The cable coils.
I bring it under, graze my back
on the roll's moist girth.
I wriggle, stand, hook it, and squirm out
onto the cool mill floor,
back among men.
The broken pillar arcs above me,
sways on its cable,
trailing splintered shadows.

I don't know yet what I'm seeing
when they set it down in sunlight
near the mill door for inspection,
analysis, and scrap, or what impressions
the roll is making on my body,
still wet and warm with its touch.

Uniform

I open my dead father's footlocker,
find his rosary in a felt pouch,
read his war diary on yellowed
scraps paper-clipped together. I put on
his Navy whites, punching my fists
through the stiffened cloth, and stand
by a mirror in tight, moldy paleness.
In a squad photo, thinned
by the heat, work, and bad food,
he gauntly holds a rising sun
flag, drooping like his tired smile
between long fingers. Before he leaves
San Francisco, he writes, *War is beautiful.*
Out where men die, men become
men. Later, he holds one of his "boys,"
Sully, eighteen, by smoldering wreckage
on a runway: *I can't stand to see any more*
of them killed. His words die out
on faraway islands of flesh and bone:
Guadalcanal, Vella La Vella,
Espiritu Santo, Efate.

Visiting Slovan, Pa.

I stand in front of my father's old house,
a small faded clapboard behind a metal fence
among all the company houses
on Railroad Street. Behind me black slag
has crept up the mountain
toward the abandoned zinc plant's
skeletal stacks. My father called Slovan
the Black Hole of Calcutta,
as if it wasn't America.

I see him running toward anyplace
that's not this house,
this town. He dreamed
of hopping a freight train
to the '32 Olympics, scrounged
the railroad tracks for coal
that fell off trains, a nickel a pail.
His sisters rode buckboards
to Atlasburg, Langeloth,
taught shoeless first graders
in one-room portable schools, paid
for his college. He returned to these steep,
shale-screed hills after med school,
the Pacific. In Pittsburgh, he opened
one office, then three.
He made my mother move
to the big house on Edgerton,
shouting, *What I want*

is always small potatoes to you.
Do I have to put that M-1 in my mouth?

Now, a small boy bangs open
the screen door of the clapboard house,
his squirt gun shooting
the air. Corn yellow hair sprouts
under his Steeler cap. Is any miracle left
for him below the black hill
and the ruined factory overgrown with weeds
Queen Anne's lace, and wild roses?
Once there was no money for Christmas.
My father cried in the steamy kitchen.
My grandmother stroked his hair, murmuring,
*Santa Claus doesn't come to poor
houses.* She cooked each child's favorite treat.
Aunt Sophie chose stewed prunes,
my father, apple strudel.

The boy turns his gun on me,
Hey, Mister, what d'you want?
Sun dazzles silver off the slag.
Just walking, I say, hoping
this boy's dad can sing
like my grandfather. He'd sit on a barrel,
a patched squeeze-box heaving
between his hands. Polkas drifted
into the dark street, and his sons,
daughters, neighbor kids, trailing home
from night games, crept near one by one.

Soon he was up dancing, forgetting
the hernia he got laying tracks
for American Zinc. On the sagging porch,
my grandfather swayed, singing:
Ain't got money. Ain't got chow.
Lots of children anyhow.

Carrie Furnace

I check the ore bin at 3 a.m. Fluorescent light
mixes with the black river. Across mountains
of ore, an orange glow flickers through slits
in the cast house roof, #4 Furnace,
an ember encased in ash. Below a metal grid
the hopper yawns, dark, empty. I put in a call
from a shed where two men doze. Outside,
a man zigzags up the steps of the ore bridge gantry,
its girders like opaque ribs against stars.
He climbs into the high crane car.
Its glinting buckets hang from cables
like steel testes on the undercarriage. Starting up,
it moves overhead, moaning on iron wheels, Jupiter
eclipsed between I-beams. The buckets drop and gush
into mounds of Venezuela-ore. Cables clack.
A bin car on the side-track fills in a few swings,
then rumbles to a stop above the hopper grid:
bottom doors bang, hiss. The load in a hot rush
thumps into the pit. I usher stuck squares
with a compressed air hose, wave
to the bin car man, set for a few hours' more.
This saurian, metal beast is the body we inhabit.
To some guys, it's a woman: *more nights*
with Carrie than the old lady. In a steel shed
there's a six-inch hole a worker torched
in the wall: outside, large red lips chalked
around it say, *Kiss me on the other side*
where spread pink thighs surround it,

through the hole, a view of the furnace.
But I look up at Jupiter, half-planet,
half-star giving off its own noxious heat
500 million miles from the sun: bloated, huffing
blob of gas and ice. I imagine this furnace
rutting the land with molten red, leaving the hills
fanged with girders and towers. Servants of steel
eros, coke-men, hookers, third helpers, bleeders,
we warm ourselves by glowing ash cans,
tend ovens in furnace greens, asbestos capes,
send 3000 degree iron down runners, catch it
in ladle cars, freeze on trestles, keep the hoppers
full of ore round the clock, the clock, the clock.
The cooling ingots on flat bed cars, dark
bell-shaped, hot at fifty yards have something
to do with our hearts after years of time cards,
swing shifts, and four-fingered palms painted on walls
like the hand-prints in the caves near Lascaux.

Cast house of #7 furnace

2

BROTHERS

*In that brief, sharp schooling, I got
personally acquainted with about all the different
types of human nature.... When I find a well-drawn
character in fiction or biography I generally take a
warm personal interest in him, for the reason that I
have known him before—met him on the river.*

— MARK TWAIN

Wing Damage

(or the assembled wreckage, bird-shaped
on a hangar floor)
for Steve

Driving home, I hear my brother's name on the radio.
The bridge arch and cables hang like a strung bow
flexed against stars: *a local pilot crashed yesterday
near Pensa—KKKKKKKKKKKKKKKK*
The car slams into the brick-clacked darkness
of the tunnel . . .

An old wind sweeps through Alabama pines, needles
scratching the salty blue of infinite space.
A path through bulldozed brush leads to a charred tree
and the hole his plane plowed into mud, dogwoods
already about the business of fall. Military school
straightened his back and shoulders, saddened his face
at the Thanksgiving table as he praised the Roman soldiers
ordered by an insane emperor to march beyond Egypt
to find the earth's edge. I wore bum's clothes
and sneered like a displaced barbarian. I remember
flower petals holed by his magnifying glass burns,
and the ferns he toppled with BB shot.
I remember him pounding the laughter out of Ray Dash
on Sterrett School's oil-soaked dirt.
I fought hard against him at army, tackle, release
because neighbor kids always picked me to even the odds
of his size and speed in the schoolyard's asphalt cages.

Later, in the car near Homestead Steel Works,
sitting in our furnace greens & hard hats,
he said, *I'll kill you if you don't go to war.*
I shouted, *Animal!* until he punched me six times
in the upper lip. My "peace" exploded into flailing
fists, wanting to hurt, both of us at the intersection,
horns blaring, his foot on the brake, the light
green. I would not walk him to the mill gate.

How many wars since Cain, back through the genes
of sorrow? How many lives fell, fractions
slower than it took his plane to spin and crash,
a shooting star through history's mad night sky?
One night in the woods, a bright streak
shot over us, a star falling. *On night patrol
you'd give us away,* he sneered. *Yelling won't
make it burn brighter.* But that streak triggered,
like the Third Law he'd always quote, a flight in me.
I stood in the clearing near the blue steel
barrel of his presence, saw a light begin
and end before thought, having no place
above earth or below stars, so it burned.
The plane's Osirian meteor dust soiled the ground
in a cone of twisted metal and the crater
left by his absence: *The pilot was half out of the cockpit,
face down in the dirt, his legs burning . . .*

Earnestine Pittman saw him crash from her shack
by the Styx River, a sign, *Bad Dogs,* in her yard:

It was wobbling. I noticed the fire
about midways of the plane. You could see smoke
boiling and the wing blew, right up in there, and pieces
went drifting. He just did get across the river.

And I still walk with him in dreams,
wading snow drifts and thickets of stunned laurel.
Grey trees serrate the white ground, sassafras,
oak, beech, maple, occasional pine. Wind shakes
the hieroglyphic twigs. Frost-coated buds whip
our faces. Deer leap into the long halls of trunks.
We walk down ravines, over intricately iced
streams, switching up hills. The forest yawns;
space, wind, trees sigh away our history,
leave only our constant breaths and dark steps
in snow. He falters, studies his compass.
Past and future lie in one circle around us,
frozen, impassive. We are lost.

Heckman And Cooley

Cooley's thin, wears bangs. Heckman
barrel-chested, pot-bellied, has huge biceps,
and his high forehead rises into a hard hat
labeled "Heck." Cooley says, on break,
Heck'll hook up steel till he drops.
He works 3 shifts: the mill, the Beer Garden
and one in bed, and with a side-glance
at Heckman, *it ain't easy to get that big.*
My job splits up their act. Two years together
and now Cooley transfers to the rolling mill,
wanting: *more pay for less work.*
Heckman faces the wide mill door,
munching: *When you're a big shot,*
I suppose your shit won't stink. I'm told
he once lifted Cooley, hung him by the belt
on a crane hook, smiled at him swimming
the air. To me, Heckman never talks, except
stay away from this fucking place, or *safety*
should be foremost in your mind. He teaches me
to guide steel hooks lowered from cranes
under stacks of metal plates. He twirls
a pointing finger to signal the crane. Eyes
on the slabs he mutters, *Take it up a cunt hair,*
then flattens his hand out lizard-quick,
when the load sways air borne
off the wooden blocks. We step back.
The slabs ascend, arcing to a rail car for loading.
Cooley jokes every chance: hunting, vacations

to Las Vegas, his wife. One lunchtime he says,
Look what the old lady gave me: his bun
crushed on a red lump of chipped ham.
The meat lies between caved-in white bread.
What's she trying to tell me, guys? He leaves it
on the table, exposed, uneaten, a stand in
for his wife. At the rolling mill, he takes me
to the orange ingot, scoops salt over it,
signals. The hot steel slides toward the rolls,
hits the water spray: *Boom*. I jump back
amid steam and his laughter. By summer's end
Cooley rarely comes. On a night in August I follow
Heckman through the maze of steel plates.
Seeing Cooley's head behind the control cage
window smeared in a red glow, Heckman surprises me,
saying more than I can know: *Cooley thinks*
he's getting out, but he's just changing
rooms on the Titanic. I smell beer.
A crane jerks overhead, lowers its claws.
Standing between thigh-high stacks of steel,
I hook my side of the load, but it lifts
too fast, tips, uncentered, swaying toward my hips.
Move! Heckman wheezes, grabbing his hook,
stalling it. I swing my legs, roll across the slabs,
the load like a steel pendulum chasing me.
I fall off into a trench, and a shadow of five tons
passes over me as the crane lifts it clear. I stare up
into angled darkness above the hung lights.
All right? Heckman asks. *Sure.* I find my hard hat
marked with a white stripe, new man.

Take a break. No need to report this, right?
Right. I walk away, to the john,
and puke out the sour burning in my stomach,
thanking him with each heave, for his huge
hands, his mountain body. For Cooley
made me laugh, but Heckman saved my legs.

The Night We Pitch It

Until the TV sails through wet, black air,
the bowling balls at the Strand
seem heavy, the linoleum floor in the cage
elevator shaved too thin. Until the TV sails
into the valley of railroad tracks, silent
as a fuse, our flat Iron City drafts
at Lasek's bore into our stomachs
and stew. A steel worker, two roofers, and a printer,
our jobs seem dead ends of our youth
that Sunday night in May when Agnole
says at the light, *I got a busted black and white*
in the trunk to get rid of. The answer
surfaces, inevitable as hills, *Throw it*
off the bridge. Until the TV booms into the empty
coal car, a shower of sparks and glass,
and we hoot and high-five, speeding off in the car
like crack high school commandos,
we aren't sure whose side time is on,
playing tackle in the mud, buttoning our nights
with Space Invaders at the Luna,
considering marriage. But there it is, that sound
filling up the deep beneath us,
and Jim shouting in the car above the rest,
By tomorrow it'll be in Chicago.

Trudging Through the Ore Yard Looking For the Supervisor's Balls

He likes to carry a golf driver
on the job, saw David Niven do it
in a war movie. When John, the foreman,
bets him he can't drive the river
from the trestle, he takes him up, sheds
his greens and white hat. We laborers
gather as an audience. He shoves a tee
in a cracked wooden block. It's sunrise.
The white balls thwack high into the blue,
arcing beyond the mountains of ore.
A few slice into dunes of iron pellets,
the reddish ore, or the chalky limestone.
Like golfing on Mars, he quips.
We cheer when he gets all of the 12th ball.
Clearing the drooped power lines,
it scratches a tiny splash
beyond the loading dock. He bows.
We admire the silly chance he took
in front of us, even his country club
golf swing. *He made it to the river*,
someone yells. The supervisor shakes hands
with men he never speaks to
except in anger. *Back to work*,
John says. *And you*, pointing to me,
you go get those balls.

The ladder curves off the trestle,
naked rungs on a stone strut. My boots
chunk into ore. I skirt the high slopes,
weave between the piles of purple pellets.
Hellenbeck steals one each day
in his lunch pail or pocket, stores them,
jars full in his garage, 15 years.
Now he could stock a furnace with his days.
The white dimpled golf balls are easy to spot
among the small, hard pellets of iron.
I find five. My pants pockets bulge.
Screw it. Let him find his own balls.
The trestle's deserted. Heaped mounds
surround me with a raw, elemental blood-smell
of wet iron ore lying in lunging shadows.
V-Ore from Venezuelan mountainsides
on my right, Montana limestone on my left.
The sun streams down like salt.
The atmosphere is a crystal geode cracked open.
The river bleeds fire and quartz.
At the fringes of the ore piles, slim stems
of chokeberry and yarrow poke up.
There's nothing between the earth and sky,
a little air, a little breath.

Luna

Crammed in an old wooden booth
at the Luna Bar, the dive of our expiring
teenage years, we shout our dreams
over "Rambling Man" blasting
on the juke box. Under the dark ceiling
lit with lonely 60-watt bulbs,
we huddle around the golden glow
of our pitcher of beer.
A necklace of bubbles rises inside
the fogged plastic. John's off to Denver
in his green Duster, to see the Rockies
and ski virgin snow. Rob's headed to Florida
for electronics school, the sun
and the women. He'll fix pinball machines
and bounce around the beach.
I say, *The mill's okay.* I'll work
a few years maybe, save, then travel
the world. *Why not?* we all say.
If we don't live in our twenties,
when will we? Stifling a yawn,
John challenges Rob to one more
game of Video Pong. They bat a white dot
back and forth across a TV screen.
We're pretending we have no parents,
girlfriends, entanglements. It's possible
under the broken squares of the cast
iron ceiling, in this Thirties bar,
to believe we'll slip through

the cracks in the Art Deco linoleum.
We know where to get fifty-cent pitchers,
one-dollar breakfasts, and jobs.
The mill's okay, I lie. I'll stay on
a few years, and then I'll have it made.

The Shipping Floor

Tonight Heckman snores in a trench
between two stacks of steel slabs
bound for a dump truck factory in Michigan.
His head lies in the bowl of his hard hat,
cushion-bands hugging his temples.
His belly rises and falls on the cement,
alien as moss on a rock. Even in summer
the air here is cool as a morgue,
conditioned by the plates of steel,
a thousand times harder than shin bones.
We grow used to the dead *clack* of chains
dropped onto them by cranes, breaking
the silence of the graveyard shift.
Heckman's half-drunk. We should be sweeping up
in the lull before the train comes
to haul the slabs away. But I'm his partner
and he's told me to watch for rats,
and the supervisor we call Vanilla Angel,
for his white hard hat and gray hair.
Vanilla makes his night rounds: the stainless
coil shop, the bar and bloom yard,
and the shipping floor. On nights when he comes,
his legs hidden by the steel stacks,
he glides toward us from the other side
of the floor. He's written Heckman up twice,
suspended him once. I imagine hooking up a load,
Heckman asleep on the top slab. We'd lower him
into a rail car and he'd wake up halfway

across the country. Blue sky and forests
would careen past him, a free wind blowing
through his hair. A dark shadow skitters
between the slabs. I toss a wooden block,
and a fast whip-tail vanishes toward the river.
The light is clear as gin; the steel, gray as ice
filled with air. Heckman draws deep breaths.
I'm staying awake, staying awake.

August Twilight Near the Hot-Metal Bridge

A rumbling diesel engine snakes toward me,
dragging five coke cars off of the rail bridge.
He leans from the caboose, waves a green light.

Across siding tracks I shout, *Tim:* a friend
lost since high school, a brakeman for Union Railroad.
Through thistle, sawgrass and ragweed I run

until he waves the lantern. The engine rumbles,
stops. Tim's built like a fireplug.
He commands trains with a wave of his hand.

His right forearm steady as a steel hinge,
he swings down to the stones. What can we say
in five minutes? He's older, has four kids.

He shows me the caboose. Benches line the walls.
His curved, black lunch pail, like a tiny barn,
rests on a table bolted to the floor. *Remember*

those wild nights in Oakland? he says. We'd cruise
the gleaming bars with our friends, but end up
drinking in St. John's Cemetery. The city lay far below

twinkling at our outstretched feet. *Hey, call. Okay.*
Then, I'm on the ties, peering through darkness
as his green light fades toward the furnaces.

Slag Pit

Skull: a crust of solidified metal formed in a ladle
by the partial cooling of the molten material —*OED*

At night the pit glows reddish,
and steams if it rains,
a trivial hell, one of many
up and down the river.
Skulls lie toppled in the pit,
dim cones lit from within,
dumped from the tulip-shaped iron
of the slag pots above.
One's nose broken off,
its gooney frustum stares,
half-buried in its own rubble.
Another points skyward,
heat waves rippling around
its varicose fire cracks.
Other skulls sniff the ground
like snouts rooting in dirt.
These are not the skulls of lost men
who dared stick their noses
where they shouldn't have,
and got them smashed off.
These are not the skulls of workers
who fell into molten steel,
their flesh transmuted to heat,
or those pinned under I-beams, or struck
by rail cars. The company's recycling.
After the skulls cool and weather,
a bulldozer crushes them
and they haul the bone-white cinders
upriver for cement stock.

Dust

I walk through motes
like a swimming creature
in a sooty sea. The thick air
haloes the halogen bulbs.
By shift's end, a coarse grit
sticks between my teeth.
Black rings circle my nostrils,
a double zero in the middle of my face.
The dust settles on the floors,
weeds, slabs, railings, roofs,
our hard hats, the thin frames
of our safety glasses, the time cards.
It smudges our names
on the card rack, combines
with grease to hard globs
blacker than cold tar on our boots.
I sweep it with a push broom
in long lines across the shipping floor.
I wonder if Irish is joking
when he says, *It's either God
or death*. Because it never stops
falling, like a slow, hazy brown snow,
sometimes I forget that it's there,
gathering in the creases of my face
and tracing the sweat-streams
on the back of my neck.

Track Gang

Our shovel blades scrape the gravel
between rails. Under steady clanks,
grunts, and thuds of dirt, we dig
to expose a rotted tie. Chug grabs
a new one off the cart. Yelling, *Macho
gandydancer,* he carries it on his back
and drops it in the stones. Its black grain
oozes creosote. Jack, the track boss,
cusses him, *Do that again, you're off
the gang. Ruin your back on your own time.*
Chug's sheepish, his face sun-cracked
and square as the eight-by-eight of wood
that we crowbar, slide and sledge
into place under the stainless rails.
Their cool silver gleams like the coins
we slide into machines, across bars
and under cages of bank tellers. All day
we bury new ties in the humble dirt
of an hourly wage where they stay
for twenty years. Together they lead
to every town in America, and end
on the blast furnace trestle.
We're paid to keep it that way.

Fatality, Open-Hearth 5

The charred man lies on the stretcher,
a burned caption to the white idea
of the infirmary room. He's on the floor
by the bed, and the room claims him now
like the words, *USS Homestead Works,*
sewn into the pillowcase. His blistered forearms
square off in *rigor mortis* against the fire
that scorched his blood-darkened face,
that tore his asbestos furnace coat
and melted the soles of his shoes.

The burned man's destroyed flesh
lies in the clean white room
to be photographed for insurance
and safety reasons, and tucked into files.
Maybe the ladle splashed the hot steel
when the crane moved, or they broke spout
too soon and the errant red-hot bath
caught him just as he turned
for the last time to eye-melting heat.

The soot-covered man has made it
to this little heaven, the one room free
of dust and grease, smoke and ashes.
No need to put him on the tightly tucked bed
wrapped in white with perfect hospital corners
and the grid of raised stitches
like a blueprint of the mill. He's gone,
though his stiff hand still creates,
in the flash of the camera, a shadow-face of grief
on the clean backdrop of the sheet.

The dead man can't stay in the spotless room,
built to reassure the union, the workers,
the wives. Its wall tiles surround him,
rectangles, neat as rail cars in the mill yard.
The stretcher's on wheels. Soon
he'll be shipped out of this narrow room
where the bed lies shrouded in white,
held up by rails of stainless steel.

Quitting Time At Homestead Steel

Fast as the hoarse steam escapes
the pipe's throat, hundreds of men run
out Amity gate to cars, bars, ball fields,
bowling alleys, diners. Their murmured cheer
fades into steady tapping, soles
of steel-toed boots, lasting 15 minutes.

Gimme a thousand Winky burgers! Smitty yells,
pushing open the glass door, his huge shoulders
draped with dirty furnace greens. They fill 3 bags.
He eats on the tailgate of his pickup truck.

Jeff's thumb and finger lift the shot glass,
like a tiny open-hearth ladle. He pours the heat,
whisky splashing down his throat. Deep inside,
burning, an ingot hardens, another day.

Hellenbeck stays an hour late, shoveling
spilled sinter dust into a hot chute.
He ambles out the deserted gate,
to the High Level Bridge, face and hair sooty
as the air when they bleed the furnace flue
into the sky. The mill roofs rise up
almost touching the bridge. The plant
fills the shoreline as far as he can see.
Flat cars clank, hauling ingots. Explosions
boom from the hundred-inch mill.
A low deep roar, like a river flowing
over rocks, is only dumped slag,
steaming and sliding down a hillside of slag.
It's quitting time. Soon he'll start
a week of 4-to-12's, then a week of nights,
then a week of days, as far as he can see.

Headlines: Found Poem

Three more steel plants to close.

Unemployed let mice out
at USS board meeting.

Steel imports reach record
levels. USS Execs told
to portray themselves as victims.

Iron deficiency in infants
linked to unemployment.

Jobless find recycling
turns garbage into 'gold.'

Last Heat

I was here, says "Pork Chop" Nickelson,
the steel pourer at Open-Hearth 5, *when 2, 3,*
and 4 went down. Drawing a long iron spoon
from the furnace notch, he pours out ten puddles
of liquid light into the dust. The steel curdles
and cools into slate-gray pucks, souvenirs
for the few old timers who've gathered
with cameras. One man's brought his teenage sons
to see the glow fade forever in the dark shed.
It's 1:44 p.m. Crane wheels rumble in high darkness
like a planet turning on its obscure axis.
A huge steel bucket hangs from chains.
Fast, faster, the cast-whistle hurries after itself
as a torrent of molten steel rushes from the spout
into the ladle. "Taps" echoes over the loudspeaker.
Soon they break spout and the full ladle,
shooting orange streaks of sputtering steel,
moves away to fill the ingot mold.
Someone whistles "Glory Hallelujah" as glowing slag
leaks from the furnace and cools on the dirt floor
like a dead river. The melter foreman
calls the last heat into the strange silence
of 11 empty furnaces: *0,3,5 sulfur,*
18 carbide, 17 manganese, copper oxide.

Ohio Underworld

Hillside lights drop mazes
of white poles into a still river.
They seem to hold up the dark.
Another world on those streets
unreels and dissolves under a sky
of water. A man I meet
beneath a bridge asks for change.
Twenty-five years at U.S.Steel,
he says. Above the flood wall,
a small orange stream trickles
from a pipe. I pour some quarters
into his hand. He nods
toward three men in suits:
I'm like the lights in the river
to them people. I leave him
standing in the runoff.

Sharpsville Quality Product Mill

A familiar orange light glows, catches
my eye, deep inside the dark mill door
at Sharpsville foundry. Shiny tracks
snake inward through the plant gate,
past *Home Sweet Home* on chain links,
past the burned, dented time clock
ensconced upside down in a cracked
ingot mold, past the guard house turned
meeting room, planning room, war
room, for workers who sat in, camped out
for months through a blizzard, bought
the place after the company'd given them
three days notice. *53% means controlling
interest*, says Jeff Swogger, CEO, pushing
his safety glasses on his nose, the screen
missing on one side. With a four-man crew
he's shoveling carbon dust into a mold
on unpaid overtime, helping the next shift.
Controlling interest in his job, his family,
and his father who raised them
on a Sharpsville paycheck. From the roof
above the orange-glowing foundry door,
a tin stack curves up, like a periscope.

"Company" John

Years later I see him, my old foreman,
now a guard, slouched in the lobby
of Duquesne's College Hall. Students
stream in and out of elevators.
I walk by without speaking, my head bowed.
You don't tell me what to do. I
tell you, he used to roar, storming
through the control room. Needles of pressure
gauges quivered above his smudged white
hard hat. At 11:15 at night he ordered
the third cast that shift, watched
a spinning bore drill into the belly
of the furnace. The third explosion
shook the dirty glass when the iron
first flowed, and he told me to shove
the black, clay cubes into the plunger gun
that plugged the hole. If we tapped before 5,
we tapped twice more before midnight; if not
it was hell in the cast house, and nobody
went near him if anything broke down. We joked
about the time he came out of the john
holding up his unzipped pants, shouting
and pointing at the first helper *to shit*
or get off the pot. He lost his job,
same as the workers when they closed Carrie
and poured water into the furnaces;
the final loads of iron cooled, untapped.

What It Takes

I've come to this bridge at night
to look at the corrugated tin ghost
of the empty mill. In river mist,
I see my dead brother's face hovering
at the edge of memory above the vacant sheds
where he used to clean the flue
at Open-Hearth 5. There's a sneer in it,
a sly smile that says, *Do you*
have what it takes?— to shovel dust
in 120 degrees, gulping salt pills,
in a job that's like war, a slow dying
of wounded in steel trenches:
orange helmets, lit molten shrapnel,
the suit coats of superintendents
bulging over hand guns.

On the bridge, an old man passes me.
Why does his face remind me
of a man in Graz, Austria,
the town my grandfather might have come from?
I'd gone there by night train
one young year, to seek the family rumor
of our origin. The man from Graz had a cane,
a thin-lipped toothless
determination. His stick clicked
off the sidewalk like tree limbs
knocking in a forest wind.
He flicked a glance at my American jeans
and green nylon backpack. I believed he sneered

like my brother, my father, and my father's
father, as I might believe
anything in a foreign town at dawn.

But tonight in Pittsburgh,
this old man hobbles on the bridge
toward the rusted streetcar cab
nailed to the outside wall of Chiodo's Bar
like a steel mask. The boards show through
its blank window, its destination,
Homestead, stamped on its forehead.
The day has forgotten Graz,
old Pittsburgh, and Big Steel,
but night might remember,
so I lean over the bridge rail
above the silent Slab and Plate Division
and ask my brother's face:
Do I have what it takes? I wonder
if we saw the same moon
back then. I can't imagine lifting,
a double-rotor Sikorsky chopper,
with fifty soldiers storing their families
in the holds of their minds, cross-winds
jostling the blades, and my hand
on the stick. Was that why he sneered?
Had he known what it takes
long before I did, that the mill would empty,
that his plane would catch fire
and crash? Did he know
that we all have what it
takes? And it takes us without asking,
and it takes us alone.

Slag pots in the rail yard, Carrie Furnace.

Last Heat is the winner of the 1999 Word Works Washington Prize. Peter Blair's manuscript was selected from 370 manuscripts submitted by American poets.

FIRST READERS:
Nancy Allinson
Fred Collins
Donald Cunningham
Ramola Dharmaraj
Patricia Gray
James Hopkins
Tod Ibrahim
Brandon Johnson
Sydney March
Maureen Murphy
Amy Ross
Marie Wehrli
Rhonda Williford
Marcella Wolfe

SECOND READERS:
J.H. Beall
Steven B. Rogers
Robert Sargent

FINAL JUDGES:
Karren L. Alenier
Miles David Moore
Martha Sanchez-Lowery, *Director*
Hilary Tham
Jonathan Vaile, *Assistant Director*

About the Word Works:

The Word Works, a nonprofit literary organization, publishes contemporary poetry in collectors' editions. Since 1981, the organization has sponsored the Washington Prize, an award of $1,500 to a living American poet. Each summer, Word Works presents free poetry programs at the Joaquin Miller Cabin in Washington, DC's Rock Creek Park. Annually, two high school students debut at the Miller Cabin Series as winners of the Young Poets Competition.

Since The Word Works was founded in 1974, programs have included: "In the Shadow of the Capitol," a symposium and archival project on the African-American intellectual community in segregated Washington, DC; the Gunston Arts Center Poetry Series (including Ai, Carolyn Forché, Stanley Kunitz, Linda Pastan, among others); the Poet-Editor panel discussions at the Bethesda Writer's Center (including John Hollander, Maurice English, Anthony Hecht, Josephine Jacobsen, among others); Poet's Jam, a multi-arts program series featuring poetry in performance; a poetry workshop at the Center for Creative Non-Violence (CCNV) shelter; the Writers' Retreat workshops and readings in Tuscany; and Café Muse at Strathmore Hall Arts Center. In 1997 The Word Works collaborated with Mica Press (Ft. Collins, Colorado) to distribute Mica's Premiere Series of literary chapbooks.

Past grants have been awarded by the National Endowment for the Arts, the National Endowment for the Humanities, the DC Commission on the Arts and Humanities, the Witter Bynner Foundation, and others, including many generous private patrons.

The Word Works has contributed artistic and administrative materials to the Washington Writing Archive housed in The George Washington University Gelman Library.

Please enclose a self-addressed stamped envelope with all inquiries. Find out more about The Word Works at:

http://www.writer.org/wordwork/wordwrk1.htm
email: wordworks@shirenet.com

Other Books from the Word Works:

Karren L. Alenier, *Wandering on the Outside*
Karren L. Alenier, ed., *Whose Woods These Are*
Karren L. Alenier, Hilary Tham, Miles David Moore, eds.,
    Winners: A Retrospective of the Washington Prize
*   Nathalie F. Anderson, *Following Fred Astaire*
J. H. Beall, *Hickey, The Days...*
Mel Belin, *Flesh That Was Chrysalis* (Capital Collection)
*   John Bradley, *Love-In-Idleness*
Christopher Bursk, ed., *Cool Fire*
Grace Cavalieri, *Pinecrest Rest Haven* (Capital Collection)
Moshe Dor, Barbara Goldberg, and
    Giora Leshem, eds. *The Stones Remember*
Harrison Fisher, *Curtains for You*
Isaac Goldberg, *Solomon Ibn Gabirol: A Bibliography of his*
    Poems in Translation (International Editions)
*   Linda Lee Harper, *Toward Desire*
*   Ann Rae Jonas, *A Diamond Is Hard But Not Tough*
Vladimir Levchev, *Black Book of the Endangered Species*
    (International Editions)
*   Elaine Magarrell, *Blameless Lives*
*   Fred Marchant, *Tipping Point*
James McEuen, *Snake Country* (Capital Collection)
*   Barbara Moore, *Farewell to the Body*
Miles David Moore, *The Bears of Paris* (Capital Collection)
*   Jay Rogoff, *The Cutoff*
Robert Sargent, *Aspects of a Southern Story*
Robert Sargent, *Woman From Memphis*
M.A. Schaffner, *The Good Opinion of Squirrels* (Capital Collection)
*   Enid Shomer, *Stalking the Florida Panther*
Hilary Tham, *Bad Names for Women* (Capital Collection)
Hilary Tham, *Counting* (Capital Collection)
*   Nancy White, *Sun, Moon, Salt*
*   George Young, *Spinoza's Mouse*

*   Washington Prize winners

Requests for our brochure and other information must be
accompanied by a self-addressed stamped envelope.